WRESTLING WITH AN ANGEL

A Story of Love, Disability and the Lessons of Grace

Greg Lucas
Cruciform Press | Released November, 2010

To my wife, Kim, whose tenacious love, forgiveness,
mercy, sacrifice, and grace is my greatest earthly
reminder of what the gospel is all about.
– Greg Lucas

CW00951902

CruciformPress

CruciformPress.com | info@CruciformPress.com

"Witty... stunning...striking... humorous and heartfelt. In our culture which is so quick to devalue life, *Wrestling with an Angel* provides a fresh, honest look at one father's struggle to embrace God in the midst of his son's disability. Can sheer laughter and weeping gracefully coexist in a world of so much affliction? Greg knows all about it. And inside these pages he passes on his lessons of grace to us. I highly recommend this wonderfully personal book!"

Joni Eareckson Tada, Joni and Friends International Disability Center

"I didn't want to read this book. I knew these tear-stained but hope-filled pages would jostle me out of my comfort zone and shake me up. C.S. Lewis wrote that he paradoxically loved *The Lord of the Rings* because it 'broke his heart'—and Greg Lucas' writing does the same for me. And it's for that reason that I heartily commend this book—especially for dads. This is just the book many of us need to taste afresh the goodness of God and the grace of the gospel even as we long for the day when this broken world will be made right."

Justin Taylor, Managing Editor, *ESV Study Bible*

"This is *not* primarily a book for parents of special needs children. Only one disability keeps a person from heaven. It is not physical or mental. It is the sin that lives in our hearts. Jake's father, Greg, is a captivating storyteller. When he writes about life with Jake, I recognize God's grace and loving persistence in my life. I want more!"

Noël Piper, author, and wife of pastor and author John Piper

"You will laugh; you will cry. You will feel sick; you will feel inspired. You will be repulsed by sin's ugliness; you will be overwhelmed by God.'s love Greg Lucas takes us on an unforgettable ride on the roller coaster of Christian experience, as he extracts the most beautiful insights into grace from the most painful experiences of life. This brutally honest and deeply moving book helps us to see that we all have special needs that only a special Savior can supply."

David P. Murray, Puritan Reformed Theological Seminary

"It is the rare book that makes much of God and our dependency on Him while also celebrating His goodness through hard things. Using his own example of parenting a child with significant disabilities, Greg demonstrates what relying on a sovereign God through extreme difficulty and suffering looks like. This book is a gift to the church, and particularly to men who need an example of masculine, Biblical leadership in the face of complex, confusing, and overwhelming circumstances. If you have ever confronted hardship and questioned God's goodness, this book provides a real-life example of trusting in the promises of God."

John Knight, Senior Director for Development, Desiring God

"Jesus told us that we must suffer with him in order to be glorified with him. All of us in Christ face different sorts of trials, but they are all shaping us up for the same purpose: conformity with Christ. In this book, Greg Lucas gives insight into his own experience of cross-bearing. A family facing disability, or those who love and minister to people in such situations, will certainly benefit from this story."

Russell D. Moore, Pastor; Dean of the School of Theology, Southern Baptist Theological Seminary; Author, *Adopted for Life: The Priority of Adoption for Christian Families and Churches*

"Greg communicates from a heart that loves Jesus deeply and does not shy away from the theological challenges his family context brings. Throughout the pages of this book, Greg has captured personal glimpses of grace in both amazing and, seemingly, mundane ways. Amazing as seen in God's sovereign hand of protection. Mundane as portrayed in what would normally be a simple task but with Jake requires great grace. It is the grace Greg has described as amazing "grace-ability," on display in their son's disability. As the father of a child with special needs, I wholeheartedly recommend *Wrestling with an Angel*."

Justin Reimer, Executive Director, The Elisha Foundation

Table of Contents

Chapters

CruciformPress
something new in Christian publishing

Our Books: Short. Clear. Concise. Helpful. Inspiring. Gospel-focused. *Print; ebook formats: Mobi, ePub, PDF.*

Consistent Prices: Every book costs the same.

Subscription Options: Print books or ebooks delivered to you on a set schedule, at a discount. Or buy print books or ebooks individually.

Pre-paid or Recurring Subscriptions
Print Book .... $6.49 each
Ebook .... $3.99 each

Non-Subscription Sales
1-5 Print Books .... $8.45 each
6-50 Print Books .... $7.45 each
More than 50 Print Books .... $6.45 each
Single Ebooks (bit.ly/CPebks) .... $5.45 each
Ebook Distribution Licenses (bit.ly/EbookLicenses)

CruciformPress.com

Wrestling with an Angel: A Story of Love, Disability and the Lessons of Grace

Print ISBN:	978-1-453818-77-0
ePub ISBN:	978-1-936760-02-2

Published by Cruciform Press, Adelphi, Maryland. Copyright © 2010 by Greg Lucas.
All rights reserved. Unless otherwise indicated, all Scripture quotations are taken from:
The Holy Bible: English Standard Version, Copyright © 2001 by Crossway Bibles, a
division of Good News Publishers. Used by permission. All rights reserved. Italics or
bold text within Scripture quotations indicates emphasis added.

One
BREAK | EQUIP

Grace breaks us with affliction in order to equip us with comfort and compassion

Blessed be the God and Father of our Lord Jesus Christ, the Father of mercies and God of all comfort, who comforts us in all our affliction, so that we may be able to comfort those who are in any affliction, with the comfort with which we ourselves are comforted by God. (2 Corinthians 1:3-4)

It sounded at first like something out of an old horror movie. I thought maybe someone was just playing around, but then I heard it again and again, a loud piercing cry, and less like Hollywood every time. The windows were down in my police cruiser on that warm fall day, but I still couldn't tell where the sounds came from. I began looking around for the unlikely sight of someone being disemboweled in a mall parking lot on a Saturday afternoon. Seeing nothing, and still hearing the screams, I called in a "disturbance." Around the next corner I found the source of the commotion.

A small crowd had their backs to me, watching what I could only imagine was a horrible fight between two grown men. As I rolled up to the scene, I notified 911 of my location and turned on my overhead emergency lights, hoping to disperse the brawl with a sudden display of authoritative police presence. Not until I exited my vehicle, ready to inflict some defensive tactics if needed, did I comprehend what was actually taking place.

Sitting in the middle of the parking lot was a full-grown man with his socks and shoes off, hitting himself in the face and screaming. An elderly gentleman was trying his best to collect the socks and shoes and get him on his feet again. But the seated man, the much larger of the two, would not be budged.

It was clear to everyone that the man on the ground was mentally disabled, and the elderly man was his father. The onlookers didn't know whether to call for help, offer help, or politely walk away. They seemed relieved that a uniformed official was there to deliver them from their paralyzing confusion.

I immediately cleared the crowd and asked the father if he needed assistance. The elderly man explained to me that he had picked up his son for a day visit from the group home where he lived.

"I knew better than to go at it alone, but sometimes he does really well. I wanted to spend

Break | Equip

some time with him so I brought him to the mall to get him some new shoes. He was fine until we got to the parking lot," said the exasperated dad. "When he gets upset he takes off his socks and shoes. His name is Donald."

At 6'3" and about 220 pounds, Donald was an imposing figure even while sitting there barefoot on the asphalt. He was in his mid 30s with a rough complexion from many self-inflicted scars. His emotions seemed to calm slightly when I arrived at the scene, but his face was still contorted with anxiety as he fumbled with his socks. Donald looked like he could handle himself all right, along with me and his father.

I knelt down to his level (even though he would not make eye contact) and introduced myself. "I'm Officer Lucas, but you can call me Greg. What's going on, buddy?"

Again the older man began nervously explaining to me what was wrong with his son. I stood up and tried to listen, but all I could focus on was the exhaustion and defeat in this father's eyes. My attention came back to his words when I heard him say in a cracked and broken voice, "I'm getting too old for this."

I guessed he was probably in his mid- to late-60s, but he looked to be nearly 80. He was tall and thin and frail-looking, white-haired and balding. He wore a dark flannel shirt and blue jeans, like an old farmer come to town for supplies. I could only imagine the hurt, disappointment, and weariness this man had experienced over the previous thirty years. But I didn't exactly have to imagine everything.

As he turned away for a moment, frustrated with the scene his son had created, the father muttered, "I'm so tired." I paused for a moment to let him regain his composure. Then I realized why I was there.

"I know what you are going through, Sir," I said, recognizing at the moment it escaped my mouth how cliché it must sound.

"You do?" he said skeptically.

"Yes, I do. I have a son just like your son. He's much younger and not nearly as big. But he has special needs like your Donald, and he throws very similar fits when he doesn't get his way. His name is Jake, and he is my life's great challenge."

I placed my hand on the dad's shoulder and smiled, "And I know you're tired."

I cautiously knelt back down to Donald's level and picked up his shoes and socks. I wasn't sure how he would react to me invading his space and I fully expected to be kicked or punched by this large, confused man. Slowly I un-balled one of his socks and began putting it back on his foot. To my relief, he extended his leg in a sort of surrender to let me know he would comply.

I rolled the sock gently over his toes to his heel and then up to his ankle. His pale, crooked feet felt cold and damp, and his long, sharp toenails were in need of a trim.

Probably true to his lifelong routine, he extended the other foot for me to do the same. Once both socks were on, I unlaced his large, worn-out tennis shoes, slipped them on his feet one at a time, and cinched them up and gave them a double-knot like I had done for Jake so many times before.

A stark vision from John 13 of Jesus washing His disciples' feet flashed across my mind, and I smiled as I thought to myself that the Lord may have had even this day and this parking lot in mind when He told His confused disciples, "What I am doing you do not understand now, but afterward you will understand."

I was beginning to understand that there was much more going on here than a simple police response to an unspecified disturbance at a mall.

Once the disheveled, child-like man was ready to get back on his feet again, I asked his dad, "What does Donald really like?"

"Chicken nuggets and coffee," he replied. I turned back to Donald and slowly but excitedly asked, "How would you like your dad to take you to get some chicken nuggets and coffee, buddy?" He gave a silent nod of approval and we helped him off the ground and into the truck.

After buckling Donald in, the elderly man returned to his side of the truck with a simple expression of gratitude. He shook my hand and thanked me in a voice drained of all emotion. I shot back, "No problem, I do this for a living."

Despite my official duties that day, I knew from experience that mostly he was thanking me because I could offer empathy and not just sympathy. Sometimes just being aware that someone else knows — I mean really knows what you are going through — is enough to bring great comfort in the midst of great despair. We both smiled with a freshly strengthened connection as I opened the driver's door for him.

Just before climbing into the truck he turned to me and said, "You know it gets worse, right?"

"What gets worse?" I asked.

"Your son," he replied. "It gets worse as they get older and you get older. They get stronger and you get weaker. You still love them the same, but it becomes impossible for you to take care of them. Even short visits become like this — impossible."

His words crushed me as I began to see myself in his weary face. I struggled to find some departing words of encouragement and hope — words for two desperate dads living in different seasons of the same struggling life.

"Grace is like that, you know," I said in response.

"It exposes our weakness in order to give us greater strength. I guess that's why we all have to depend on someone a little stronger than ourselves." At the moment, it was the best I could do.

"Yeah, I guess so," he replied contemplatively as he shut the truck door. "Thanks again, friend," and he drove away.

As the two men rolled off the parking lot in the old pickup truck, I watched the weary dad lift his arm and place it around the shoulder of his disabled son. A prodigal never finds love so satisfying and sweet as he finds it in the unconditional arms of his father.

I returned to my police cruiser, drove to the far end of the parking lot, and fell to pieces, wrestling hard against the tears of stored-up emotion liberated though this unexpected encounter. Through force of will I soon regained my composure, hoping no one had glimpsed this tough, stoic, in-control cop crying like an infant.

The thought of it ever getting any more difficult absolutely devastated me. As hard as it had been, I had always clung to the hope that someday it would get better; someday it would get easier. I lived with an unspoken assumption that someday Jake would learn to use the bathroom, someday learn to communicate his needs, someday be less frustrated, less combative, less compulsive, less confused. That someday I would be able to hold it all together and be the dad I ought to be for Jake.

The cold, hard truth had hit me like a storm. It might actually get worse.

My body will get older and weaker and Jake will get bigger and stronger and more defiant. His needs will increase as my abilities to care for him decrease. No matter how frail I get, Jake will never be able to care for me — it will never be that way with us. Jake will always need to be taken care of, and someday I will not be able to give him what he needs.

I hear religious-minded people all the time say with good intentions, "God will never place a burden on you so heavy that you cannot carry it."

Really?

My experience is that God will place a burden on you so heavy that you cannot possibly carry it alone. He will break your back and your will. He will buckle your legs until you fall flat beneath the crushing weight of your load. All the while He will walk beside you waiting for you to come to the point where you must depend on Him.

"My power is made perfect in your weakness," He says, as we strain under our burden.

Whatever the burden, it might indeed get worse, but I know this — God is faithful. And while we change and get old, He does not. When we get weaker, He remains strong. And in our weakness and humility, He offers us true, lasting, transforming, and undeserved grace.

It is this grace that enables us to do more than survive in this world. Grace enables us to thrive in the presence of this world's sufferings while magnifying the One who breaks us with affliction—that He might equip us with comfort, compassion, and strength to give to others.

In the midst of this deep, celestial moment, I realized I had just experienced a divine appointment. This was not just a providential assignment for an empathetic police officer sent to help a weary father with his disabled son. This was more, a lesson of grace that would stay locked in my own heart until I would need it most in the months and years to come.

And I would need it.

In response, I stood for a moment on holy ground praising the God of mercy and comfort, asking for more strength and grace for the future with my own son. My worshipful hymn and prayer of praise sounded like this:

> Blessed be the God and Father of our Lord Jesus Christ, the Father of mercies and God of all comfort, who comforts us in all our affliction, so that we may be able to comfort those who are in any affliction, with the same comfort with which we ourselves are comforted by God.
>
> (2 Corinthians 1:3-4)

Two
DISPLAY | REVEAL

Grace displays our sin as in a mirror, but reveals the cross as through a window

In this is love, not that we have loved God but that he loved us and sent his Son to be the propitiation for our sins.... We love because he first loved us. (1 John 4:10, 19)

The alarm goes off inside my head usually a few moments before the clock on my nightstand sets in motion the events of the morning. It is amazing how the mind and body can synch to a scheduled stimulus response, almost to the minute, each and every day.

It's 5:58 a.m., and I have two minutes before my morning routine begins.

I watch the clock and wait for the alarm. It's not a desire for more sleep that holds me in place. Nor is it the comfort of my blanket on this crisp, cold, dark morning. I take refuge in my bed for these few peaceful moments to think about my life.

I reflect on my weakness and inability to meet

the demands that have been placed on me through the circumstances of my journey. I wonder why God's plan for my life includes so much frustration and hurt. Then I question why God even has a plan for me at all as I contemplate my sin, self-centeredness, pride, and constant sense of failure.

Suffering seems to be the tool He uses to draw me close. But the very affliction of my soul and the anxious weariness of my heart, things that should force me to run to the light, often drive me furiously into the darkness.

I know He loves me and cares for me, but sometimes I cannot understand this strange affection. What kind of love is it that brings so much pain into my life—especially from a sovereign being who has the power to make all things right. And so, by nature, I resist the One who ultimately has designed all these difficult conditions for my good and for His glory.

It's 5:59 a.m. I want to turn off the alarm, go back to sleep, and wake up in a different place and time. I want to wake up a better man, or in different circumstances, something other than what's right here, right now. I am exhausted already, simply by anticipating the next twenty minutes. Guilt begins to disguise itself as conviction, and so I pray.

Father, forgive me for my sins—cleanse me from all unrighteousness. Make the cross of your Son visible

*for me this morning as I approach this day. Show me
your greatness in the smallness of my life. Lord, I am
helpless against what is before me this morning, and
I do not know what to do. But my eyes are on you.
Please wake my son gently and peacefully. Create
in him a good mood and a cooperative spirit. Give
him an understanding of your love. Give me an
understanding of your love. Ease his frustration and
help me get him out of bed, cleaned, dressed, and off to
school. Create in me the heart of a father, that I might
be the man my son needs me to be. Make me more like
Jesus. None of this will be possible unless you intervene
in my life and my family this morning. Lord, before
my feet touch the floor, give me strength and grace—
especially grace. I am desperate for your grace...*

The shrill tone of the alarm clock pierces my
thoughts and brings an impromptu *amen* to my
prayer. A bit startled, my heart begins to beat faster,
pumping much-needed blood into my reluctant
extremities, a slight injection of adrenaline to assure
the job gets done.

Strength and grace, before my feet touch the
floor. Its 6:00 a.m., and I'm ready for the fight.

✵ ✵ ✵

Almost every morning I have to restrain my son
physically. To get him out of bed, change his diaper,

and clean his body usually requires a degree of sheer, measured force. When he was small this was easier. But now Jake is the size of a small man, and stronger than some full-grown men. He is long and muscular, strong and lean. When he was born six weeks premature in the Neonatal Intensive Care Unit, he weighed less than five pounds. But this morning his large feet jut out from underneath his covers and hang off the edge of the bed, and a dangling arm rests a loosened fist on the floor.

I try to rouse him peacefully by gently rubbing his long, warm back beneath his t-shirt, speaking soft words of sweet affection. I usually know within the first few seconds whether it is going to be a "good day" or a "bad day." Sometimes he wakes gently and allows me to continue this display of affection, stirring slowly and quietly. Those days are rare. Most mornings he resists, pushing me away and protesting my invasion of his rest with a loud, high-pitched, piercing whine that shatters the morning peace like a rock through a window.

After physically raising him from his bed and placing his feet on the floor, I begin the dangerous duty of undressing my teenage son—shirt off, pants off, socks off, diaper off. His whining increases as I remove the clothing, partly because he knows what's coming next, but mostly because of the sensory integration disorder that brings misery with his nakedness.

Placing Jake on a towel in the middle of the floor, I begin cleaning the excess mess from his backside to make the impending bath as sanitary as possible. This necessary action increases his sensory overload, amplifying his verbal protests and producing a violent thrashing of his long, powerful legs. It's not that Jake likes being dirty. He just hates being cleaned.

By this time, my sweet wife is usually standing in the bedroom doorway, awakened by the noise of the morning ritual. Her presence is always comforting. She comes to encourage me, and to try to calm Jake with a quiet, pleading tone. She also comes to help with the next phase.

Two people are needed to bathe our son. It's not wise even to try if you're alone. You might be able to begin the process by yourself — and on rare occasions you can even complete it — but you nearly always need to call in your backup at some point. One person to hold Jake in the tub, the other to scrub him clean. Most mornings there is much to scrub. Human fecal matter can dry hard as plaster — one item from the "Things Nobody Should Have to Know" vault of my life. Contained inside the diaper, it is usually not too much trouble. Matted in hair, packed under fingernails, or even coating the teeth, is quite a different story.

After bath time it's back to the bedroom floor

where lotion is applied, clean clothes are fitted, socks and shoes are put on and cinched up. Next, I lay Jake down on the floor again. Kneeling, I straddle his body and pin both his arms securely but gently against his body between my knees. I sing a calming song while I brush his crooked teeth—straining to hold him down and get the job done.

Much of this same routine is repeated after school, then after dinner, and then again just before bed. While not every change of clothing and cleaning of the body requires a bath, every single attempt at personal hygiene comes with a fight.

Many times while cleaning and changing Jake, I have been kicked in the face, bitten, smacked, clawed, spit on, or hit with flying objects. It is not too unusual to come away from one of these cleanups with a bloody lip or a new scratch. Every attempt to prepare him for the day becomes a violent struggle played out on several levels, my best intentions pitted against his greatest resistance.

Many mornings I leave Jake's room dejected, hurt, and emotionally drained. Many evenings, in desperation, I find myself restraining his struggles by wrapping him in my arms against his will and gently whispering, "I love you. I love you. I love you—no matter what."

How do you care for someone who resists your love with violence, who opposes your very presence

even when that presence is necessary for his good?
How do you keep on loving when the person you
are devoted to seems incapable of affection? The only
way to make any sense of this kind of relationship is
to experience it through the truly unconditional love
of the Father.

Much like my son, I have been disabled all
my life. My disability affects everything I am and
everything I do. Scripture diagnoses this disability
as sin. Not individual acts of sin, but a sin nature, sin
residing within my heart. It causes me to reject love
and embrace fear. It plagues me with a slumber that
makes me strangely satisfied to lie in my own filth
and not be disturbed. It's not that I like being dirty. I
just hate being cleaned.

But God is patient, kind, and full of grace. He
knows how I am made, but He does not excuse
it. He refuses to permit my life to take its natural
course. He has sacrificed much to make me His son,
and He will not stand by when I am in need—even
when I resist His compassion and care.

In my son I see a picture of my own relationship
with God. In Jake's defiant refusal to be loved,
cared for, and washed, I am reminded of the cross.
There, the violence of divine love overpowered my
rebellion and forced upon me a process of cleansing
redemption that I did not want to undergo. In some
ways the process is still ongoing, and most days, I

still resist. In my persistent disability I fight against the transformation being worked in me. But I face a power greater than my own and a love stronger than my rebellion. It is as if a bloody, beaten, crucified Savior wraps me in His arms, subdues me with His affection, and whispers in my ear, "I love you. I love you. I love you—no matter what."

Three
ROUTINE |
SURPRISE

Grace surprises us with God's presence in the
details of our daily routine

And from his fullness we have all received, grace upon grace.
(John 1:16)

"Flip a coin."

"What?"

"Rock, paper, scissors?"

I joke with my wife in a humorous attempt to
decide which of us will take the lead tonight on bath
time for Jake.

"I'll do it," she replies, with a slight resignation in
her voice.

"No, I'll do it," I say, responding to her weary
tone.

Such a mundane decision for most parents is,
in our home, an act of heroism. One of the most
powerful phrases in our love language to each other

is, "I'll give him his bath tonight." Admittedly, Kim has told me "I love you" many more times than I have told her.

As I begin to walk up the stairs to Jake's bedroom I roll up my sleeves and literally stretch my shoulders, back, and neck to prepare for the match.

I can hear that he's watching TV, flipping through the channels in a rhythmic pattern. The calming effect that the television has on Jake is amazing. Even more amazing is the predictable evaporation of his composure whenever I turn off the TV and start to run the bath water.

I have never bathed a cat, but I know what it's like to bathe a cat—even a family of cats, because I have bathed my son for seventeen years. It's not merely that Jake does not like to get naked, or that he despises being cleaned. He also fears water. The sound of a filling bathtub is the sound of terror to Jake. Running water might as well be flowing lava to his sensory integration disorder. Combine nakedness, running water, and cleaning, and the result is an epic battle—two each day, one in the morning upon waking and another in the evening, usually around 7:30.

Halfway up the stairs, my mental focus intensifies and the physical strategies begin sorting themselves out in my mind. I know exactly how it's supposed to go:

*Gloves on, water drawn, towel covering the floor,
clothes off
butt cleaned, fight on, in the water, scrub down
wash hair, rinse hair, out of water, towel dry
lotion, commotion, tears like the ocean
dressed again
done*

It's like a strange, familiar rap song inside my head. Actually, rap music would be more inviting to this born-and-bred West Virginia boy than the commotion I am about to hear.

Maybe I'll listen to the iPod tonight. Put on the noise cancellation headphones and turn up the music to drown out the wailing and gnashing of teeth. There is something inspiring about human drama played out to the right soundtrack. I imagine my life paired with a Norah Jones blues beat or, perhaps more fitting, a Bob Kauflin spontaneous hymn. Music often brings me some peace in the midst of my chaos. But tonight God will play His own song—a love song that will make much of His mercy and magnify His grace.

Truth is, you never know when or where the breeze of God's blessing is going to blow. Grace is like that—unexpected, undeserved, and unpredictable. Tonight God will reveal some of that mysterious grace in the peacefulness of His presence—and at bath time, no less.

As I reach the top of the stairs the wind of God's grace blows through our home. It is there for us just as it was for Moses when he stood before the Red Sea, just as it was for Joshua at Jericho, and for Gideon at Jezreel.

The TV goes off and, to my utter amazement, Jake voluntarily, with a smile, walks into the bathroom and begins to get undressed—on his own. He is prancing around the bathroom like a two-year-old wearing his father's shoes.

Miraculously, his pants are not soiled. There is no wiping or fighting. I run the bathwater and he steps in without being coaxed. He motions for me to put some bubble bath into the water and the tub quickly fills with suds. He's happy tonight. It's going to be a good night.

Then Jake does something I have never seen him do. He lies back in the water and relaxes. He really relaxes. The ticks and twitches all but stop as he lies quietly in the warm bath. His face is not contorted with stress. He does not whine. The room is perfectly quiet.

Taking advantage of this rare moment, I just sit there and look at my son. He looks different tonight, almost like he has no disabilities at all. His glasses are off, his eyes are clear, and for this moment the torment of anxiety has left his face.

The refraction of the light through the water

makes his legs look straight and strong. His complexion is perfect in the soft glow of the bathroom lamp, and for the first bath in a long, long time, his demons are cast out and replaced with a tranquil peace.

I stare at Jake for several minutes, imagining what he would look like or be like without his afflictions and handicaps. For a brief moment I am given a picture of my son without his disability. It is a wonderful gift from a gracious God.

He stays in the bathtub until the water cools. On his own, he stands up to be dried off. As I wrap the towel around him and lift his 130-pound body from the water, I embrace him tightly.

He shivers slightly from the transition but allows me to hold him longer than usual. I smell the strawberry shampoo in his hair and the clean scent of soap on his cheek.

"Thank you," I whisper in his ear. "And thank You," I whisper in His ear.

Grace, even in the small things of life, is never small grace.

Four
OPPOSITION |
HUMILITY

Grace humbles us by crushing our pride through humiliation

Clothe yourselves, all of you, with humility toward one another, for God opposes the proud but gives grace to the humble.
(1 Peter 5:5b)

I used to pray for humility in raising Jake. (I tried praying for patience once but that was a disaster.) Then I discovered that humility almost comes naturally when you're dealing with disability. It just shows up when you need it. Sometimes it even shows up when you think you don't need it. That's usually when you need it most.

I am by nature a very prideful person. I care deeply about my appearance, my work ethic, and my reputation. Jake is by nature a pride killer. I love that about him—not often at the moment, but always in retrospect. I love that about him because, especially in his disability, he has a unique capacity to be used as a vessel for God's glory and as a messenger of God's grace for my greatest good.

Truth is, we are often so self-centered that we fail to notice the most significant and God-glorifying aspects of what's taking place around us. We miss out on a lot of human joy and deep inner satisfaction because we are so tied up with personal cares. But Jake can shift my focus away from my superficial concerns and force me to reflect on what is most important. As I am caught up in the reality of his limitations, I am reminded of how small and secondary most of my personal concerns really are.

When humility comes in like this and exposes my self-focus, I want to be able to see it for what it is: a loving gift from the grace of God. But humility is a gift that's hard to receive, because it often comes by way of humiliation, which in the eyes of the world and my own fallen, human wisdom, is nothing but weakness and failure. Throughout the Bible, though, God uses weakness to define strength, and He uses humility to display greatness. Whether it is a stuttering goat herder who takes on an Egyptian Pharaoh and leads a nation to the Promised Land, or a small boy slaying a sword-wielding giant with a sling and a stone, weakness is God's tool to shame the strong. And when the King of the universe became a man—even the servant of men, laying down His life for the very sinners that spit in His face—humility displayed greatness like the world had never seen.

* * *

When Jake was 6 years old we visited a large church in Louisville, Kentucky. At that age, despite his leg braces and diminished mental capacities, Jake was very charismatic, fully mobile, and rather mischievous.

Even for the average family, visiting an unfamiliar church can be a daunting experience. Add children and the pressure increases. Add a disabled child like Jake and you never know what will happen. I admit that oftentimes I enter a new church with a bit of an attitude. I assume that they won't know what to do with my son. I assume that I know more about disability than they do. I assume that this will be another bad experience, making it impossible for me to focus on worship.

This is one of the ugliest forms of pride in my life. The truth is, usually the only obstacle barricading my heart from true worship is my own self-centered arrogance. On more than one occasion, God has used my son to tear this barricade down and expose my soul to sweet humility. This was going to be one of those times.

We took Jake to the children's pre-school class with the other kids and settled into the pew for some good edification from a well-known pastor and preacher. So far this church was passing all my tests. About a quarter of the way into the sermon, when no usher had yet called me back to the nursery to pick up my son for an early departure, I finally relaxed enough to worship.

Thinking to myself that this might actually be a good church visit, I slipped my arm around my wife, loosened my tie, and basked in the rare moment of normalcy. I focused in on the preacher and opened my ears to the message, eager for good news and practical application. But perhaps what was most important for me that day was to have my assumptions addressed, assumptions about a particular kind of church experience I thought I deserved.

As I watched the preacher, my gaze was drawn to a door off to the left and behind the pulpit. The door had opened slightly and the Children's Minister was peeking through. This was the same lady who a few minutes earlier had greeted us warmly, taken Jake by the hand, and assured us, "Don't worry, he'll be fine." She seemed to be studying the choir area that stood on a raised section several feet behind the pulpit where the pastor stood, preaching.

It soon became obvious that the Children's Minister was searching for something. *Or someone*, I thought to myself. Scanning the choir area, I found what she was looking for. The soft red hair of my son slowly began to appear above the empty chairs.

Enter humility.

As our six-year-old rose up like an angel in a Christmas pageant, every eye in the congregation fixed on him. Jake, knowing he had gained the best seat in the house and captured the attention of the entire 800-person church, stood fully upright, crossing his arms and beaming like a conquering hero.

The Children's Minister began gesturing to Jake, trying to coax him towards the door without drawing any more attention to this spectacle. But Jake wasn't giving up his spot for all the animal crackers in preschool.

Somehow our son had managed to position himself directly behind the preacher and, from his perch in the choir seats, just a bit higher. As every eye fell on Jake, it must have seemed to the pastor, busy delivering his sermon, that the congregation had suddenly become unusually attentive. He had no idea what was unfolding just a few feet away, no idea that every person in that church was actually looking right past him.

As the efforts of the Children's Minister to persuade my wayward son grew more frantic, the congregation began to snicker. When the poor woman got down on her hands and knees and crawled between the rows of chairs in an effort to capture Jake, the snicker turned into a steady, rumbling chuckle. As Jake casually maneuvered down the aisle to the next row to avoid interception, the chuckling got louder. When Jake raised himself up to his full six-year-old height, sternly crossed his arms, and shook his head as if to say, "No way, lady," the rumble from the congregation turned to open laughter.

The pastor, understandably, had been growing more and more uncomfortable as the congregation's response to his sermon grew more and more inexplicable. Like a good preacher, however, he discretely checked his fly and kept pressing on.

At this point, I was probably the only person in the church less comfortable than the perplexed preacher. From the moment I had caught sight of Jake, I'd been trying desperately to ignore what was happening. Sinking lower and lower into my seat, I was looking around for the nearest exit when my wife finally elbowed me and said quietly, "Go. Get. Him. Now!"

I rose from my pew and, like a repentant sinner responding to an altar call, I somberly walked the aisle to the front of the church. As I climbed the steps to the stage I looked up at the pastor—who by this time may have thought that something Pentecostal from the Book of Acts was unfolding—gave him an assuring nod, and pointed to the choir loft.

"That's my boy."

The good minister looked behind him. Taking in the entire fiasco with a glance, he turned back, nodded and smiled at me, faced the congregation, and returned to his text. The man hardly missed a beat.

Retrieving my prodigal son, I led him back in the direction of the nursery. As we began to exit, stage right, Jake blew a flurry of kisses to the congregation, eliciting another round of laughter. As we left the stage we both waved farewell. I imagine my wave displayed a good deal more ambivalence than Jake's.

But a strange thing happened to me that Sunday. Instead of grabbing my family and marching out of the sanctuary, we stayed and I was humbled. I was humbled because God had used my son to expose my pride before 800 laughing people. I learned to laugh a lot that day, also.

We ended up becoming members of that church, friends with the pastor and his family, good friends with many in the congregation, and best friends with the Children's Minister. She also, through God's grace, became one of Jake's closest advocates during the three years we lived in Louisville. We still keep in contact with her today, and still laugh together at all Jake's humiliating antics and pride-destroying accomplishments.

* * *

Not all our stories of humiliation end so happily. Sometimes life with Jake isolates our family and repels others, forcing humility upon us in a far more challenging way. But the lessons of grace are still there to be learned, and even these most difficult trials can produce a smile of humble amazement—at least in retrospect.

Once, when Jake was about 13, we were attending one of my youngest son's Little League Baseball games. Jake was sitting in the crowded stands between Kim and me when we gave each other our coded look of panic that says, "Oh my goodness, what's that smell?!"

As Jake's face turned from beet red to ghost-rider pale, I grabbed his hand and attempted to persuade him to walk with me out of the stands. When he stood up, a flow of brown, rancid liquid began pouring out the bottom of his shorts onto the bleachers.

My mind flashed back to a crowded public swimming pool several years earlier. Standing in the pool at the bottom of the slide, surrounded by about 20 preschoolers and soccer moms, I was trying to coax Jake down into the water. I watched in horror as the water coming down the slide turned brown. Like a scene straight from *Jaws*, mothers grabbed their children and fled the pool in a thrashing, splashing panic. It was not the first or the last swimming pool we have shut down.

Back at the ballpark, I tried to get Jake's mind off of the "Code Brown" and onto evacuating the scene, but it was too late. As his ultra-sensitive sensory integration kicked in, the odor triggered his gag reflex and he began to gag and vomit.

When scenes like this are played out on home-field advantage, we are usually surrounded by families who know us and accept Jake. Often times these people jump right in and help. At the very least they know how Jake is and they just keep on watching the game as if nothing has happened. But this was an away game.

As Mount St. Jacob erupted from both ends, people began dispersing like it was a terrorist attack—some in anger, not knowing my son had underlying issues, and some just out of uncomfortable fear. This only added to Jake's embarrassment, resulting in a fit of temper in which he began biting himself and screaming uncontrollably. In desperation, I picked up my fully grown teenage son, threw him over my shoulder, and carried him out like a wounded soldier from the battlefield. I retreated to the car and then home for the cleanup while my wife stayed for the much tougher HAZMAT decontamination of the bleachers.

Sometimes the process of humility is just plain humiliating.

Society perceives humiliation as an ultimate failure to be avoided at all costs, but of course, God can use it for our ultimate success. He accomplishes meekness by crushing our pride in order to lavish us with the eye-opening gift of true Christ-like humility. And it is here, as we find ourselves covered in the stench of our pride, that the aroma of grace smells the sweetest.

I often wonder what it would be like to be a normal dad, of a normal family, with a normal son. I sometimes imagine sitting through an entire church service or ball game or date with my wife without having to answer an urgent alarm activated by Jake. I would probably have more friends, more time, and more worldly accomplishments. I would definitely have more pride.

In exchange, there would be less opportunity to recognize the amazing grace that God displays each and every day through the disability of my son. It is this grace that humiliates my pride, humbles my soul, deepens my shallowness, and allows me to see what is most important in life.

I am grateful that humility comes naturally with disability—I don't even have to pray for it. It just shows up when I need it most, or when I think I don't need it at all, which is usually when I need it most.

Five
GIFTED | SAVED

Grace saves us by freely and undeservingly giving
what we need to be saved

*For by grace you have been saved through faith. And this is not
your own doing; it is the gift of God, not a result of works, so that
no one may boast. (Ephesians 2:8-9)*

The more I try to comprehend the sovereignty
of God in salvation, the more I am astounded by
His grace. Even the faith to believe the gospel is a gift
given to those who deserve only His just wrath.

Jesus came to this earth as God in the flesh,
lived a perfect life, and died a sacrificial death. All
the wrath of the Father justly reserved for us was
cast upon His Son for the just payment of our sin.
All the righteousness of Jesus is transferred to us
through His sanctifying work on the cross. As John
MacArthur has put it, "On the cross, God treated
Jesus as if He had lived your life, so He could treat

you as if you had lived His." After dying a sacrificial death, Jesus was buried in a tomb. Three days later, He rose again in eternal victory over death.

This is the gospel. This is God's plan for His glory and for our eternal good. Through this gospel we obtain eternal life in order to experience His glory for all eternity. All of this is obtained by grace through faith. Those who place their trust in this gospel are counted righteous in Christ, before God the Father.

But how is this applied in the life of an individual who cannot respond in faith or who does not have the ability to comprehend the basic truth of the gospel? I'm not thinking of the native in a distant, unreached part of the world, someone who at least has a general revelation to point him towards more specific revelation. I am thinking about my 17-year-old son, who literally has the mental capacity of a 2-year-old.

Many Christians approach this sticky theological topic with their feelings, bypassing biblical study in the fear that truth may not be as comforting as their emotions. We want to believe that infants, very young children, and mentally disabled people are basically innocent in the eyes of God. Should they die without having attained a certain degree of mental capacity, we assure ourselves, they are necessarily saved from His wrath. Certainly this is how God would do it, right? This rationalization feels good and makes sense to our hearts.

But is this biblically accurate? Do our feelings and desires in this area line up with Scripture? What about those who have a deep personal investment in this theological question? Can an appeal to emotion, a vague pointing in the general direction of God's love and mercy and grace, provide genuine, faith-filled comfort?

What I really mean is, what about those of us who love people like Jake? What are *we* supposed to believe?

When it comes to such crucial theological questions, I have found that feelings are a weak salve to the hurts of my heart. Obscurities also fail to give hope. If children are saved because of their innocence, at what point do they become accountable? When they understand the basic outlines of the gospel? When they "know the difference between right and wrong"? When they begin to recognize the true depravity of their hearts?

The questions become even more difficult in regards to the mentally incapacitated. At what IQ level does God begin to require someone to respond in faith to His gospel in order to be saved? How much faith is enough faith? If a mentally disabled person steals something and knows it is wrong, is this sin? How is this sin dealt with by a holy and just God? Does He sweep it under the rug of the universe? Who sets the guidelines for these answers? How can any real confidence be found in a human assessment of who is innocent and who is accountable?

Sometimes, lost in a storm of continually unanswered questions, blown all over an ocean of uncertainty and fear, of heartaches and joys, I can be shipwrecked by my own desperate emotions. I cry out for something more solid and trustworthy to take hold of, something to keep me from drowning in the unknown.

And I receive it. Solid biblical truth and the grace to understand it is the most comforting gift that God has given to me as Jake's father. Yes, there is mystery. But there is enough sturdy truth in God's Word to keep me afloat.

Here is what this solid truth tells me.

I have had a problem with sin since before I understood the saving gospel, even well before my capacity to understand it. I was conceived in sin (Psalms 51:5), and sin has been bound up in my heart since I was a child (Proverbs 22:15). Even the intention of my heart has been evil from my youth (Genesis 8:21).

So I was dead, disobedient, and doomed in my sin, unable to respond on my own. I was known by God as a son of disobedience. By my very nature, He saw me as a child of His wrath, just like the rest of unsaved humanity (Ephesians 2:1-3). I was hopeless and helpless.

Not too comforting so far, is it? To be honest, it's closer to terrifying, for whom then can be saved? The spiritually dead may be helpless. They may even be ignorant. But they are not innocent. It would seem, therefore, they are doomed.

But go further into biblical truth and there is comfort. There is real hope. This hope rests, not in self-sufficiency, but in the power of God's rescuing grace, in the power of a strength sufficient to breathe life into dead bones, a strength that can cover my sin with the cleansing life-blood of God's Son.

So the bad news is that we are all born guilty. But the good news, especially for people like Jake, is that we are all born helpless, too.

In ourselves we are, every one of us, powerless to understand, comprehend, or respond to God's plan of salvation. One instant before God brought me under the power of gospel conviction, I was no more capable than Jake of understanding the gospel, regardless of our IQ differential. If I am going to be saved, if Jake is going to be saved, if an infant or the comatose or sufferers of dementia are going to be saved, we all have precisely the same need. We must be *raised* from spiritual death, *given* a new heart that loves and desires God, *given* a new mind that treasures the gospel, and *given* saving faith in the sacrificial death of Christ for our sins. There are no active verbs in that process. They are all passive verbs.

I'm not sure in what order these things take place. Perhaps it is all so instantaneous that it cannot be differentiated or separated accurately by our finite minds. What I do know is that all of it happens by the undeserving grace of God through the redeeming work of Jesus (Romans 3:23-24).

Maybe now you are starting to see why I can have a realistic hope for Jake's salvation. What I may never have, it's true, is the kind of compelling evidential proof, the external markers of a real faith and real Christianity that children of God often perceive in one another. That kind of evidence requires a certain emotional capacity, an ability to interact personally that Jake will never possess. He will never have the tools to display, in any sort of typical way, a life of genuine faith in God.

But the fact is that, in the grand picture of God's rescue, Jake is no different than me. While I may have more cognitive capacity to understand the gospel, I am still just as mentally handicapped as my son in the eyes of God. Actually I am more than mentally handicapped: I am dead. The same grace that awoke my dead heart and gave eternal life to my decaying bones can accomplish salvation in the heart and mind of my disabled son. That's what the Bible tells me. That's what gives me comfort.

* * *

In summary, salvation happens by grace. Ultimately, we can't do a single thing to bring it about. This does not mean, however, that I am passive about Jake's spiritual condition. I am to be diligent with each of my children's spiritual nourishment. But, as with physical nourishment, we do not feed all our children the same way.

For our two strapping teenage sons, we simply set the plate before them and they devour every scrap (and usually ask for seconds). Our 4-year-old daughter still needs her food cut up and cooled off, so that's how we prepare it for her. Jake sometimes needs to be spoon fed, but we make sure he eats well on those days, too—equally good nourishment, just with a simpler and more accessible presentation.

The same holds true for the gospel. I am responsible to prepare the gospel for my children, to plant the seed of faith, and to water it accordingly. God is responsible for their understanding and growth.

I realize that this illustration is not all-encompassing. Some people are unable to understand any form of gospel explanation. Babies die at birth or in the womb, having never comprehended human speech. But that same biblical truth serves as a source of comfort even for these extreme circumstances of God's mystery.

David told of his relationship with God from before birth (Psalms 22:9-10). John the Baptist was said to have been filled with the Spirit even in his mother's womb (Luke 1:15). And who could read Psalm 139, especially verses 13-16, and not see that God is intricately involved in our lives even as our molecular structure begins to form in the darkness of the womb? In God's design, helplessness is not the same as hopelessness. To loosely paraphrase Augustine, *God gives what God requires.*

If my son needs faith to be saved, then God, in the great mystery of His sovereignty, will give him the necessary faith at whatever level he needs it. But it will still be given with the same grace that is given to me.

I do not rest assured in my own salvation because I am trusted with obtaining it, perfecting it, or keeping it. That would be most detrimental to my assurance. Instead, I rest in the grace of God that He is in full and absolute control of my eternal destiny—from before the foundations of the earth, and continuing on through my birth, life, death, and eternal state. This is where my hope comes from. This is my comfort.

And this is my comfort for my son.

But God, being rich in mercy, because of the great love with which he loved us, even when we were dead in our trespasses *(even when we were mentally disabled)*, made us alive together with

Christ—by grace you have been saved…and this is not your own doing; it is the gift of God. (Ephesians 2:4-5, 8b) (parenthetical addition mine)

I'm sure there are many more points that could be argued and applied on this matter. But I have a personal investment in it: the life of my own son. And so in the end I will trust the One who has a personal investment in me, through the death of His own Son.

To God be the glory.

Six
SATISFIED |
WAITING

Grace satisfies our heart with answers to prayer
while we wait for the ultimate answer

*Now to him who is able to do far more abundantly than all we
ask or think (Ephesians 3:20a)*

One of the longest patterns of recurring
intercessory prayer in my life has been directed at a
single goal: that my son might be able to speak. If I
could heal just one aspect of his condition, if I could
give just one gift to address his physical ailment, it
would be the gift of speech. Most of his frustration,
and much of our collective family frustration, comes
from Jake's inability to communicate effectively on a
regular basis.

Sometimes we don't know Jake is sick until he
is very sick. We don't know how badly he is injured
until bones show up broken on an X-ray. We don't

know he is sad until he begins to cry uncontrollably. We don't know he is angry until the remote control, or his eyeglasses, or a soft drink flies across the room and crashes against the wall.

At home, these forms of miscommunication are burdensome and exhausting. Out in public they can be downright dreadful and even dangerous.

Once, at a fast food restaurant, Jake was sitting quietly with us at the table eating, when all of a sudden he looked panicky and began to turn pale. As I glanced over at him, his teeth clenched hard, but no sound came from his mouth. Not knowing if he was choking or having a seizure, I jumped up and ran around the table to check him out, only to find that his fingers were caught in the hinge side of the heavy glass entry door he was sitting next to. Jake's inability to talk, mixed with his extremely high pain tolerance, produced four flattened fingertips before I even knew anything was the matter.

Later, I felt sick to my stomach as I tried to imagine what it was like to need rescuing, to have your rescuers sitting across the table from you, and for them to be utterly unaware because you cannot even say, "Help!"

Jake's inability to communicate well can also lead to misunderstanding. This, too, can be dangerous in public. When the large, hulking gentleman sitting in the row in front of our family at the movie

theater gets a Big Gulp drink poured on his head
because Jake has gotten mad over a scene in the
movie, miscommunication can lead to the kind of
misunderstanding that may be hazardous to my
health. It has happened.

So, for years, I have prayed that God would give
my son a voice.

I long for my son to have peace in his frustrated
heart. I also wish for tranquility in my sometimes
discouraged home. But one of my greatest yearnings
on earth is to have a deep conversation with Jake.
This is just one of the things that, for me, will make
heaven especially sweet. I have so many things I want
to tell him and, more importantly, so many things I
want to hear from his heart.

I have waited and waited for God to answer this
prayer. At times it seems like heaven is brass to my
plea. But the longer I live, the more I realize that in
God's merciful ways and grace-filled applications,
He has sent me many answers, even as I wait for the
ultimate answer.

I asked God specifically to give Jake words. God
graciously granted five.

Jake's entire spoken vocabulary consists of
"Dah-dah" for Daddy, "Momma" for Mommy,
"Maw-maw" for his grandmother, "Dad-dad" for
his grandfather, and "Ho-ho-ho" for, you guessed
it, Santa Claus. And yes, we hear about Santa Claus

all year round, and we encourage and cherish this because it is an answer to my prayer.

Beyond those five vocal expressions, there are no other words in Jake's audible vocabulary. But there are some necessary signs. Jake can sign words like *Jesus, Bible, Shoes, Play, Please, Sorry, Candy, Drink,* and *Eat*.

There is also some very beautiful singing. Jake loves to stand in church with an open hymnal—or anywhere, for that matter—and sing. His singing consists of one long baritone note that he can hold for a surprisingly long time. Over and over and over. It sounds a lot like Gregorian chant.

He also loves to carry a Bible and pretend he is reading, using the same long baritone sound that he sings with. Because he is standing and holding a Bible instead of a hymnal, perhaps he is preaching. God knows what's going on there, even if I do not.

There are other nonverbal forms of communication Jake has developed over the years. He communicates best and most profoundly through body language. A stubborn and slightly rebellious "*No!*" is communicated by repeatedly crossing his arms, looking over his glasses, and breathing heavily out of his nose, sort of like a snorting horse. This is Jake's form of posturing, and is usually followed by an emotional outburst of some kind.

If this specific body language leads to him biting his forearm, we know that some type of violent behavior will quickly follow. When this happens, I take off his glasses—usually the first thing he throws—and try to clear the area of any other likely projectiles. While we very much discourage this type behavior in Jake, I don't get too upset when he does it because at least he is trying to communicate. This, too, is an answer to prayer.

On the opposite end of the spectrum is the celebratory, *"YES! I really approve of this moment!"* This is signified by Jake raising his arms in triumph, jumping up and down, and yelling loudly—very loudly. His victory dance usually appears when he is at his happiest. It is wonderful to see on Christmas morning or at a birthday party or when one of Jake's favorite people, his Maw-maw, comes to visit.

He also does his victory dance after accomplishing something significant. Completing a 50-meter race at the Special Olympics or going to the bathroom in a public restroom nearly always trigger the victory dance. So does making it through an entire elevator ride without puking.

Closed-in spaces like elevators make Jake insanely nervous. But *exiting* a closed-in space represents a victory over one of his greatest fears. To see him burst from an elevator like an NFL player celebrating a game-winning touchdown is quite an experience. So are the looks we get, especially from our fellow passengers who had no idea how exciting elevators could be.

Jake may be non-verbal, but that does not mean he's quiet. I thank God for every victory dance. My son's noisiness is an answer to my prayer.

Then there are the precious ways Jake communicates affection physically. When he is happy and wants to show his love, he hugs. As our 4-year-old daughter would say, "He squeezes the choke out of me."

For our daughter, being embraced by her much larger brother is more like a headlock than a hug. This can be confusing for a little girl who loves her disabled brother very much, but doesn't completely understand why discomfort has to come along with his expression of affection. Actually, Jake intends for his hugs to be a sort of headlock, because his goal in wrapping his arms around your neck is to lower your head and finish the hug by placing his mouth directly on your hair in the form of a big, wet kiss. Jake has always had oral sensitivity stimulation issues with hair.

So while Jake's hugs can be a little messy, somewhat confusing, often very loud, and even a little painful, when you leave our house with a sore neck and a big wet spot on the top of your head, you know you are loved.

Remember how Jake blew kisses to the congregation? That may have seemed like pure, innocent affection at the time, but these flurries have a specific meaning for Jake. They are essentially about ushering you out of his space. They are his way of being lovingly polite while communicating either, "You've overstayed your welcome, don't let the door hit you on the way out," or, "I've had enough of this place, I'm out of here!" It's one of the most genuinely amusing things Jake does. His sense of humor is a treasure to us. A treasure and a great answer to prayer.

Finally, there is God's gift of electronic communication devices. Jake uses a handheld computer with a picture touch-screen that can communicate all kinds of phrases. When talking on the phone with him you might hear a mechanical voice saying: "I love you," "I miss you," "I want to go to Maw-maw's house," or "Is it almost time for Santa Claus to come?"

For me, all of this illustrates the difference between *an* answer to prayer and *the* answer to prayer.

Our sovereign Lord has the ability to grant anything we ask at any time. He is generous and kind and loving and cares for us beyond our wildest imaginations. We can be assured that when we are genuinely hungry and ask for food, He will give us bread and fish, not stones and snakes. But sometimes, if we ask for steak and shrimp, bread and fish may not seem like the answer we were looking for.

I think the appetizer is meant to increase our desire for the main course. Such has been the case in my own prayer life. My heavenly Father, in His infinite wisdom, has answered all my prayers for Jake—with glimpses of the greatness to come. He has granted a foretaste of His glory by revealing the shadow of His coming blessings.

We still live in a fallen, sin-stained world. Even the best things here are mere silhouettes of what God has in store for us on that day when sin is no more. But we can be assured of this—He has more in store for us than we could ever think to ask for (see Ephesians 3:20).

The full answers to our prayers and the full glory of God's blessings will only come in eternity—and then, they will last for eternity. But for now, informed by Scripture, and full of Godward faith and biblical hope, our anticipation of what's to come protects us from trusting in the temporal things by keeping us longing for the eternal things. In this life it is vital and necessary that, to one degree or another, we remain dissatisfied. The tension is that, here, all our prayers are answered, but all our prayers also await ultimate answers.

Today I communicate with my son through a few important words, some necessary signs, a sophisticated electronic device, and some rather charismatic body language. God has given me an answer to my prayer.

But I dream of a day when Jake and I sit quietly and stare into each other's eyes for a long, precious moment. Broad smiles flash across our faces in silent communication of overwhelming joy. It's a smile shared only by the close bond and affection of fathers and sons.

Then the silence is broken by Jake's voice, "Dad, there are so many things I have wanted to tell you."

"I know son, I know."

This is *the* answer to my prayer. And it will be worth the wait.

Boekell Photography

Seven
DARKNESS |
RESCUE

Grace pursues us into the darkness of our
hopelessness carrying the rescuing light of the
gospel

*Indeed, we felt that we had received the sentence of death. But
that was to make us rely not on ourselves but on God who raises
the dead. (2 Corinthians 1:9)*

Jake was born in the Neonatal Intensive Care
Unit where my wife, Kim, works as a registered
nurse. Kim took care of Jake for the first few weeks
of his life. During that time, a handwritten note
was placed on his isolette. The baby boy had been
"abandoned to Social Services" by his birth mother.

Skipping over a very long and miraculous story,
we adopted Jake and brought him into our family.
I was 25 and Kim was 22. We had just celebrated
our fourth wedding anniversary and had no clue of

the pain and desperation that was coming our way. Neither did we know at the time how God would use this sovereign adversity to mold us into the family we are today.

As we began our parenting expedition, everything was fresh and bright, with all our hopes and dreams in clear focus before us. We jumped headlong into the role of father and mother and lived it to the fullest.

Kim met with other young mothers and showed off her new baby boy, while I bragged to all the guys about my amazing son, prophesying of a strapping young man proficient at handling himself, as well as handling every shape of ball that any sport might provide.

I envisioned long walks where I would share my fatherly wisdom with my son. We would talk about school and dating and cars. We would go hunting and fishing and be as close as a father and son could be.

But God had a different plan and a different route for our journey. It was a plan that would reveal our weakness—as well as magnify His greatness—in ways we could never have imagined. During this time, we would voyage to the darkest corner of our desperate insufficiency, the place where God's light of rescue would shine the brightest.

* * *

Shortly after Jake's first birthday, Kim took him on a walk to visit her sister a few blocks away. He was riding in one of those infant backpack carriers and enjoying the trip. It was a beautiful spring day.

Arriving at her sister's house, Kim greeted her sister and their father, who was also visiting. Turning his attention to Jake in the backpack, Kim's dad saw that something was very wrong. As Kim took the carrier off for a better look, she was instantly horrified by Jake's expressionless face and dark purple lips. Her son had stopped breathing.

In a mother's panic, Kim picked Jake up and frantically called out his name, but he was unresponsive and unconscious. Kim instinctively began administering choking drills and CPR, but still nothing. In the ambulance on the way to the hospital, Jake did show signs of consciousness, only to stop breathing again, turn blue, and appear lifeless.

I received a call over my police radio briefly describing the situation. I raced across town in my cruiser with lights flashing and sirens blaring. Arriving at the hospital, I found Kim holding Jake in her arms, crying hysterically and calling out his name over and over while nurses administered drugs through an I.V. in his arm. It was a scene I will never forget.

Neither will I forget the feeling of helplessness as I stood there in full police uniform. The beneficiary of all the training and authority the city could grant, possessed of gun, badge, and bulletproof vest, I could do nothing to help my own son. I stood frozen in fear, powerless and numb.

After Jake was stabilized and medicated in the emergency room, he was admitted to the pediatric ICU for observation and testing. By now Kim had had time to think, and she knew exactly what was going on. The doctors confirmed her diagnosis when they told us Jake was suffering from apnea-related seizures.

One minute he would be alert, happy, and healthy—and the next minute he would stop breathing, go limp, turn blue, stiffen out, appear dead…and then wake up crying. The process repeated every few hours. During the seizures there was absolutely nothing we could do to get Jake to breathe. It just had to run its course.

While in the hospital, Jake was sedated and hooked up to every tube, wire, cord, and machine imaginable. But even with all the medical technology available, the doctors still could not tell us what was causing the seizures or how they could be stopped.

The medical staff finally sent us home with a monitor to track his heart rate and breathing, along with some medication they hoped would control the seizures. I remember, during those first few nights at home, hovering over Jake's crib watching him sleep, waiting for the breathing monitor to go off and the seizure to set in. It was like waiting for death and then trying in vain to chase it away. We took turns guarding our son throughout the night.

I vividly remember one such night, standing guard in Jake's room as he went into a seizure and stopped breathing. As the apnea alarm unleashed its high-pitched scream, I held my own breath to try to experience first-hand what my son was going through. After about a minute my lungs were burning. At ninety seconds the need for oxygen overpowered my will. I gasped for air, placed my face on Jake's chest, and began to sob while the seizure ran its course. His face turned pale white, his lips dark blue. He looked lifeless. And I was hopeless.

For many nights thereafter we would be awakened from dead sleep by either the apnea monitor or the heart-rate alarm. They sounded like smoke detectors, and triggered about the same reaction in us as waking up to find your house on fire. Still today, as I look back, I can feel the tightness in my chest and the pain of disappointment, hopelessness, and stress as the seizures went on day after day, night after night.

* * *

Kim and I were so young, and the whole parenting role had just kind of fallen into our laps. We hadn't really known what to expect, but we could never have expected this.

We arranged our schedules to work on opposite shifts so that at least one of us could always be home with Jake. We would pass each other in the doorway with a momentary hug or kiss, and a report of how many seizures Jake had suffered in the other's absence. Most of the time we were too exhausted to make much sense of anything.

Jake's medical problems had begun just before we finalized his adoption and placed him on our health insurance. This meant, of course, that none of the medical expenses related to his "pre-existing condition" were covered. As the bills began to pile up—very quickly—so did our anxiety.

The seizures continued for a year. We took Jake to every doctor and medical specialist we could find. It seemed like every time we shuttled in and out of another hospital or doctor's office we came away with a new drug, a new theory or diagnosis, and a fresh rush of anticipation from the possibility of a new solution. Nothing worked. Heart-wrenching disappointment hit us time after time, as the seizures continued to drag our son to the edge of death.

By this time Jake was in a perpetual stupor. His happy, bubbly personality had been wiped away by the unrelenting seizures and the side-effects of multiple drugs. In its place was a constant state of dazed lethargy. Kim and I weren't much better off.

That's when the grace of God came to us in a whole new way. In the midst of this dark season, Kim and I both came to the very end of our strength, our hope, and ourselves. It was there in a pitch-black pit of desperation that God showed up with the light of the gospel. It wasn't until years later that I realized He had been there all the while, orchestrating the seemingly tragic events of our lives into a perfect love story of grace and redemption.

When Kim and I were married we both considered ourselves to be Christians. We went to church on occasion, believed in many Christian values, and even prayed sometimes at night. We both had bonded leather Bibles with our names printed in gold leaf on the front. They looked rather convincing lying closed on the end tables of our living room couch. We even possessed certificates of baptism and were on a membership roll at our local church. But there was little, if any, saving evidence to our professed faith.

To make matters worse, I was an unusually strong-willed man and took great pride in my ability to fix whatever might be broken. I brought my police mentality into every situation: Find a remedy, implement it, problem solved. I had been taking this approach for a year now with my son, driving him to doctor after doctor and coming away with medication after medication. *We will fix this*, I told myself. But nothing could fix my son.

Then one day Jake's seizures started early in the morning and continued throughout the afternoon. It was the highest volume of seizure activity we had ever seen, and he was fading fast. In desperation we took him to the doctor's office. While he was seizing in the waiting room I approached the nurse's station.

"Can someone please help my son?!" I asked in tears and anger. The doctor brought us back, looked at Jake, and prescribed yet another medication.

"Try this," he said.

"And what if *this* doesn't work?" I replied.

The doctor paused for a moment and then confessed, "I am all out of options. I really don't know what to do with your son."

We drove home, silenced by despair and wondering if we would soon watch our son die. I had left all my strength, hope, and confidence at the doctor's office.

That night, as I sat in Jake's nursery waiting for the apnea alarm to go off, I had a horrifying epiphany.

I cannot help my son. The medications cannot stop the seizures. The doctors do not know what to do.

I fell to my knees on the floor of Jake's nursery

and cried out to God. I don't remember exactly
what I said, but I do remember coming to the end
of myself and begging Him to take over—not
just Jake's illness, but my entire life. A few nights
later, while we lay in bed, Kim told me of a similar
experience she had had, crying out to God in
desperation, asking Him to intervene in her life, our
family, and our son's illness.

We repented of our pride and turned away
from the false hope of our own strength. We banked
everything we had, everything we were, our lives, and
the life of our son, on the gospel of the One who had
given his very Son to ensure our healing and hope.

From that point forward we approached life and
our son's illness with faith and trust, not that God
would miraculously heal Jake—although we prayed
He would—but more importantly that God would
be our salvation and strength through this life of
difficulty He had so mysteriously planned for us.
Less than a month later we went to see a pediatric
neurologist who specialized in seizure disorders.
This wonderful doctor took one look at Jake,
prescribed one medication, and the seizures stopped.
They have never returned.

I would love to write, "And they lived happily
ever after," here and end the book. But while God
had finished this chapter of our lives by saving us and
our son, there would be many more chapters of grace

to write as He continued our story. The seizures were gone. Our hearts were changed. The crushing burden of trying to live under our own strength was forever removed from our backs. But we soon found out that our struggle was only beginning.

Jake was now two years old and functioning like an infant. He could not speak, walk, or feed himself. Some of his bubbly personality returned, but the seizure medication still overshadowed his true character. New diagnoses would come. Every specialist we saw would add something new to the spectrum of possible disorders. Simple Seizure Disorder was followed by Cerebral Palsy, followed by Sensory Integration Disorder, Obsessive-Compulsive Disorder, Pervasive Developmental Disorder, Non-Otherwise Specified (whatever that means), and finally Autism.

To this day, no one is quite sure what's wrong with Jake. But I know what is right with him. He is my son. And not only did God see fit to bring this exceptional child into our family, but He used Jake as a miraculous messenger of saving grace.

When people ask me how I became a follower of Jesus, I always tell them that a two-year-old, non-verbal, mentally disabled, autistic boy led me straight to the cross and since then has been used to display God's grace in the most amazing ways.

Eight
PROTECTED | IMPERILED

Grace protects us through danger, not always from it

See that you do not despise one of these little ones. For I tell you that in heaven their angels always see the face of my Father who is in heaven. (Matthew 18:10)

I do not believe Jake has a guardian angel assigned to protect him from harm. I believe he has a Father who sits on His throne in heaven surrounded by an army of angels who intently watch the face of their Commander. With one nod of the Almighty's head, a legion of angels can be dispatched with unimaginable speed to preserve and protect. Night and day they wait, watching the Father's face as His eyes watch over my son. I believe it is God who watches, not any created being. And it is God who supplies whatever help is needed.

Jake's care is not delegated.

* * *

Our house has always been like a fortress, locked down with dead bolts, door chimes, and alarm systems, keeping Jake from escaping into a world where danger lurks and disaster awaits. But locks and alarms can offer a false sense of security from both unpredictable circumstances and sovereign providence.

When Jake was 4 years old he nearly drowned in the creek that borders our property. Kim was spending time with our three toddling sons in the back yard while tending our small vegetable garden. She bent down to pull some weeds, and then turned to find only two boys. She scanned the yard in panic. "Where's Jake!" Noah, also age 4, pointed toward the creek and replied, "Jake's swimming!"

The creek was only about a foot deep, but apparently Jake—who could barely walk at the time—had tumbled down the steep bank and landed in the rocky stream. An instant later, Kim looked over the bank and saw Jake motionless and face-down in the water. She leapt into the water and pulled him out. His lips were turning blue and his skin was cold to the touch. It had been almost two years since the seizures had stopped, but here Kim was again—holding in her arms a son with no breath in his lungs and apparently no life in his body.

Kim administered CPR while screaming for help to whoever may have been driving down the road 10 yards away. No one heard her cry. At least, it appeared that way.

Suddenly Jake coughed, and what seemed like a gallon of water came out of his mouth. He gasped for air and began to cry. And there on the creek bank a young mother embraced her son, receiving him back from certain death.

There would be many more scenes of traumatic danger and divine rescue during Jake's childhood. Some were more spectacular than others, but each one left us with a profound sense that there was much more going on in the unseen realm around our special son than what we were aware of.

One afternoon, Kim and I had just returned home from the grocery store. I was taking the dog for a walk while Kim was unloading the groceries from the car. It was one of those instances of miscommunication: each of us thought the other had Jake. In fact, Jake had circled the car just out of our sight as Kim and I moved away from the car in opposite directions. A minute later, seeing me with our dog in a field across the street, Jake began to follow after us.

There's a bend in the road near our house that creates a blind spot for drivers. The speed limit is 30 mph, but most people drive 45 or 50 mph. I was only in the field a short while when I heard tires screeching in the road behind me. I spun around and this is what I saw.

A huge Cadillac sat motionless in the middle of the road. Behind the wheel was an elderly lady. She was frozen in position, staring straight ahead, eyes bulging, arms locked at the elbow, her hands in a death grip on the steering wheel.

A few inches from the front bumper of her car stood Jake, wobbling slightly in his leg braces and looking at the car with curiosity and confusion. The whole scene had an otherworldly feel to it. It was as if, just for a second or two, someone had pushed the pause button on space and time, averting a tragedy that would have rippled through many lives.

Indeed, Someone had.

A few months later, our dog was struck and killed by a car in the same spot.

✣ ✣ ✣

Then there were the falls. Stiff leg braces, mixed with a lack of fine motor skills, added to severe cognitive delay often made Jake look like an intoxicated clown on stilts. What made matters even worse was Jake's seeming inability to use his arms to break his fall. A simple stumble could easily turn into a face-planting, full-body impact, a lumberjack's tree crashing into the living room floor.

The Emergency Room staff knew us well during those days. Jake suffered at least three concussions, ten staples to the back of his head, a broken nose, a chipped tooth, two black eyes, a fractured elbow, and a broken foot. He was almost always bruised and knotted. If not for me being a police officer, Kim being a nurse at the same hospital, and the treating physicians knowing our family and Jake's disability, I'm sure we would have been flagged for investigation by the Child Welfare Department.

I could go on describing Jake's brushes with disaster, with every partially told tale probably making Kim and I look worse and worse as parents, but the truth is that all children are susceptible to danger. Disabled children are even more helpless and sometimes even more difficult to protect.

Still, we know God gave us Jake to love and to care for, yet all these injuries happened to him while he was close by us. Whenever the guilt over this fact grows especially heavy, one passage becomes my confidence. Second Corinthians 1:10 reads, "He delivered us from such a deadly peril, and he will deliver us. On him we have set our hope that he will deliver us again" (and again, and again, and again!). God in His sovereignty and omnipotence is fully aware of every danger, hazard, and peril that lies in wait for my son. And He has delivered Jake through every one of them.

My faith in God's promises is not naïve. I know from Scripture and experience that it is always dangerous to be God's child. We seek to exercise simple dependence on God's ultimate deliverance, but along the way pain, suffering, and sometimes even death become ways in which God can be most glorified in our difficult lives. The Bible teaches that while grace will not always protect us *from* danger, it will always carry us *through* danger.

That's why my confidence comes from the promise that God will forever be present to care for and love my son with a divine compassion that outshines my best abilities and most hopeful intentions as an earthly father.

God's compassion never sleeps, His care is always diligent, His eyes are ever attentive, and His love will forever exceed Jake's most intimate needs. God is on His throne at this very moment. At His feet, legions of angels are poised for dispatch.

My Father has His eyes on my boy, and the angels have their eyes on the face of my Father as they watch and wait for the Commander's nod.

Nine
RELEASED | GRIPPED

Grace peels back our fingers to reveal God's greater grip of grace on our fragile life

For we were so utterly burdened beyond our strength that we despaired of life itself. Indeed, we felt that we had received the sentence of death. But that was to make us rely not on ourselves but on God who raises the dead. He delivered us from such a deadly peril, and he will deliver us. On him we have set our hope that he will deliver us again. (2 Corinthians 1:8b-10)

All I could think about as I lay there in our bed was the old man I had met in the parking lot earlier that day. I saw again his weathered face, weary from battling the demons in his disabled son. In the dark, his words haunted my memory. As he climbed into his pickup truck to take his son for chicken nuggets and coffee, he had turned to me and said, "You know it gets worse, right?" The conversation replayed in my mind.

What gets worse?

Your son — it gets worse as they get older and you get older. They get stronger and you get weaker. You still love them the same, but it becomes impossible for you to take care of them...impossible.

It was all becoming painfully true.

As Jake had entered his teenage years, especially after puberty set in, something had happened, something had changed. He became very aggressive, constantly anxious, and openly defiant. His obsessive-compulsiveness increased dramatically while his social abilities nearly vanished. By the time he turned 14, Jake's personality had been almost completely transformed. There were still small glimpses of the happy, bubbly kid we once knew, but his character had taken on new, unwelcoming aspects.

We have two other teenage boys, so I know the enormous physiological and personality changes that follow when the male teenage brain is soaked in testosterone. But with Jake, something else was going on. He began to develop involuntary tics and severe bi-polar mood swings. The doctors prescribed various meds, but all that did was add horrible side effects. Even his schoolteachers noticed the personality changes, and as Jake's social withdrawal grew worse it became more and more difficult for him to advance in his special education classes.

With a child like Jake, there is no promise that

things will ever get better. As Jake moved into his teen years, what we were seeing in him was typical: usually the challenge becomes greater as the child and the parents grow older. Still, there is always the hopeful thought that someday, somehow, things will get easier. But it wasn't going that way for us. After 21 years of marriage and 17 years of parenting, everything was becoming more and more difficult.

Our son was now regressing at an alarming rate and the entire family was in a state of constant stress. Our other three children were walking on eggshells in our home, never knowing what would set Jake off or trigger his next fit of anger. The more weary and stressed Kim and I became, the more it affected the atmosphere of our entire household.

Home should be a place of refuge, a safe place where a family can retreat from the tension and trauma of life. But our refuge of rest was quickly becoming a dwelling of despair. Before long, we all began looking forward to work or school as an escape to something more peaceful. In those days it was actually less stressful to work in the ICU or as a police officer than to be home when Jake was there.

As the husband, dad, and leader of my family, I took it on myself to keep Jake's emotions in check, to deal with his violence, and to protect the rest of the family from any fallout due to his unpredictable behavior. Schedules were rearranged, plans were cancelled, friends stopped coming over, and I soon became almost totally consumed with this effort.

I'm sure that more than a few people were willing to help us during this volatile time, but I refused to ask for rescue. The smallest white flag of surrender was to me a symbol of failure that my prideful heart would not allow me to hoist.

Meanwhile, my health had begun to decline and my mental state was deteriorating almost as quickly as my son was regressing. My blood pressure was high, my energy level was low, and I was terribly out of shape—physically, mentally, and spiritually. I became depressed, anxious, and achingly bone-weary, but my pride would not let me loosen my hold on the wheel of this sinking ship.

Doctor after doctor, psychologists and psychiatrists, continued to offer advice, therapy, and always more medication for my son. In sinful desperation, I found myself leaning away from the presence of an eternally capable God and placing my feeble trust in the best doctors or the newest drugs. This counterfeit hope began to diminish as Jake continued to get worse.

I had always thought it would be an honor to care for Jake for the rest of his life. That had been the plan since we first understood the severity of his disability. I would devote my entire future to meeting his most intimate needs, no matter how great they might become. But Jake's ever-increasing opposition, his violent resistance to the most mundane of daily activities, had broken me. I was already defeated, and the worst part was that I refused to acknowledge it, refused to release my grip.

The climax came one day in a psychiatrist's office as Kim, weeping from anxiety, tried to explain what we were going through with Jake. I sat nearby, anesthetized by despair, Jake fiddling in the seat next to me. The doctor listened wordlessly, took some notes, thought a moment, scribbled out a prescription, and uttered a phrase we had heard countless times: "Why don't we try this…"

That was my limit.

Sixteen years. Scores of medical and mental health professionals. One indistinguishable office suite after another. And that same phrase at the end, hundreds and hundreds of times. *Why don't we try this…*

"Are you listening to anything my wife is telling you?" I said. My approach was quiet, but direct and austere. As I continued to speak, however, something rose up in me. I was not going to allow this to be just another pointless visit to someone who might as well be an accountant or an auto mechanic for all the good it was doing us. I have often been extremely grateful for the medical profession. But at that moment all I could think was that someone playing at being a doctor, and merely adding another twist to the endless, maddening riddle of prescriptions that had become Jake's life—that was not going to cut it this time. I was determined to drive home the seriousness of the situation and reach this doctor's seemingly calloused heart. As I leaned closer to her desk, my voice grew louder and my stare grew more intense.

"The pills don't work—they make things worse. Nothing you or any other doctor has done in the past three years has worked. We are *desperate* here. Our other children are suffering. Our home life is under duress. This child is in a state of constant misery. He needs help. We need help with our son."

Her reply literally stunned me.

"I'm not sure what you want me to do. If you'd like, I could call social services and have your son placed in emergency foster care. You could waive your rights as parents and turn him over to the care of the state."

The room was silent. Kim and I had just enough presence of mind to realize it wasn't safe for us to open our mouths or even to think about what to say in response. I stood up and took Jake's hand, leading him out of the room without acknowledging the doctor. It wasn't polite, but it was probably the wisest course of action at the moment. "I'm finished here," I said calmly to my wife as I walked towards the door. Kim just sat there, still in shock over the doctor's words.

As Jake and I exited the office and passed by the receptionist's booth, a man sitting in the waiting room began to stare curiously at my son. Jake was emitting a high-pitched whine, something he does in strange and stressful situations, such as this highly unusual display of emotion from his dad. Most days I ignore the rude stares and the discourteous whispers. Most days I walk away telling myself that people just don't know any better. Today, obviously, was not like most days. I turned toward the man who was staring and stopped mid-stride, venting loudly through my clenched teeth and glaring at this unfortunate scapegoat of my frustration.

"Can I help you with something?" I shot at him as I took a step closer. He turned away and hung his head like a scolded puppy. I slowly scanned the waiting room, glaring in turn at each averted face.

"This is my son!" I said to my captive audience, with barely controlled anger. "He doesn't like it when people stare at him. I don't like it when people stare at him! He has some problems, okay? But then again, don't we all."

I paused, waiting to see if anyone would dare to break the awkward silence. No one did. Turning quickly toward the exit, I continued out to the parking lot, fumbling for my keys and placing Jake into the truck. I had just unleashed my fury on a waiting room full of patients at a psychiatrist's office.

They probably thought I was the one in need of help. This was a new low point.

Suddenly the worst parts of our life with Jake flooded back into my mind. The seizures as a baby, the shriek of the breathing monitor in the middle of the night, the sleeplessness, the emergency room trips, the brushes with death, the anxiety and hopelessness and a thousand forms of utter helplessness. What was God doing to us? Why was He allowing us to suffer like this? How could the worst of the past be happening all over again?

As I was buckling Jake into the back seat, Kim opened the passenger door of the truck and tried to talk me down from the ledge of my anger. "Calm down," she affectionately reassured me. "It's going to be alright."

"I wish I could believe that," I replied cynically, holding back tears of anger and bitter disappointment.

"There is a place called The Potomac Center," she said as she took her seat next to me. "They have a school that works on behavior and self-help skills for kids like Jake. I think we should look into it." She handed me a brochure.

The Potomac Center was at the opposite end of our state—a five-hour drive from home. Kim told me there was a long waiting list to get into both the center and the school. It was also a full-time residency. Why was this better than the ludicrous option of foster care that the doctor had suggested? The drive home was long and silent. Many things ran through my mind. Few of them were godly or good.

Back at home, I locked myself in my study. Folding my arms on top of my cluttered desk, I lay my head down, finally and openly broken. I vividly recall asking God to take my life, thinking how easy death must be compared to all the suffering and heartache of the past few years. But like so many times in my undeserving existence, instead of sending death, God sent grace. The grace that brought the gospel of hope into our hearts sixteen years earlier would once again, through much suffering, prove faithful and amazing.

True desperation is always the most fertile ground for God's grace to produce an abundant harvest of hope. And each time God has shown us His greatest glory, He has always first revealed our greatest despair.

I am not one to implore the Lord to speak to me, open a Bible at random, and blindly place my finger on a passage of destiny. Yet I am very much aware of His voice in the written Scripture, and of the power of His providence to place the right words at strategic moments before my obstinate mind and feeble eyes.

This day He would choose the 3x5 card taped to

the side of my bookshelf with the inspired and timely words of 2 Corinthians 1:8b-10:

> For we were so utterly burdened beyond our strength that we despaired of life itself. Indeed, we felt that we had received the sentence of death. But that was to make us rely not on ourselves but on God who raises the dead. He delivered us from such a deadly peril, and he will deliver us. On him we have set our hope that he will deliver us again.

I reached for the index card, my Scripture memory verse for the week, and tore it from the tape holding it to the old bookshelf. On the flip side of the card was this quote from Pastor John Piper: "God is not like a firefighter who gets calls to show up at calamities when the damage is already happening. He is more like a surgeon who carefully and skillfully plans the cutting He must do and plans it for good purposes."

My grip began to loosen, more from involuntary surrender than from hopeful anticipation. But God was gently prying away my fingers to reveal His own hand of sovereignty, strength, and protection.

Letting go is always difficult. For parents, one of the most anxious, heartbreaking moments is when your child must be released into the world to take his or her own way in life. It is not simply the prospect of independent living that we find frightening. It is knowing that as we send our children out, life will inevitably serve up lessons involving failure and danger and risk. But when that child is severely disabled and entirely dependent on your care, guidance, protection, and nurture—a child who has no voice, no ability to defend himself, no way of negotiating through these lessons of life—letting go seems more like the malpractice of accidental amputation than the outcome of a successful surgery.

But Kim and I have learned that faith means deciding, acting, and committing to a course of action without fully understanding how things are going to work out. We also know that it is not our faith that contains the power to deliver—it is the object of our faith that both holds the power and determines the outcome. And when you see that the object of your faith is greater than anything in the universe, letting go is no longer the same thing as giving up.

Beneath the death grip of every parent holding tightly to their special child is the strong, reliable, and gentle hand of a Father who will never let go— the Deliverer, the Surgeon, the reliable object of our faith. Suffering reveals our need, and our need reveals the Savior. He will direct your life in whatever way is necessary to loosen your grip—not to take something away, but to make possible more than you could have ever hoped for or imagined.

This is the grip of grace.

Ten
FUTURE |
PRESENT

Grace walks with us into the future, revealing the
unknown darkness as the shadowing presence of
our Father

*It is the LORD who goes before you. He will be with you; he
will not leave you or forsake you. Do not fear or be dismayed.
Deuteronomy 31:8*

Jake left on a Thursday towards the end of
winter. Outside it was bitterly cold and spitting
snow. The wind was stretching pinkish-grey clouds
across the skyline as the sun struggled to make its
morning appearance.

I woke early after a mostly sleepless night and
stood by the doorway of Jake's bedroom. As I
watched him, my memory was in overdrive. It seemed
as though every significant moment leading up to this
day was jostling for attention at the same time. One
memory in particular took hold, focusing me.

Wasn't it only yesterday that I would come home from work early in the morning, get Jake out of his crib, warm up his baby formula, and hold him like he was part of my own body? Sitting in a dimly lit room in absolute peace, watching my son as he watched me, his eyes glued to mine as he took his bottle, both of us speaking in deep, father-son conversation without ever saying a word — the future had looked so very different back then. But now, standing there in the hallway in the shadows of the past, I found a familiar presence, an urging of the Spirit that led me into quiet pleading for this most difficult day.

Lord, he is your boy. He was your son long before he was mine. Hold him tightly from this morning on, like you have so faithfully carried him all these years. Help him to understand how much we have loved him. More importantly, help him to understand how much you have loved him. Protect him from harm and provide him with favor wherever he may go. Give us an awareness of much grace this morning; we are desperate for your grace.

Kim met me in the hallway and we gently woke our son, helping him out of bed and onto the floor for his morning change. He resisted a little, but not like usual. It was as if he was aware of our heartbreak and had compassion for our weakness. I gave him one last bath, combed his hair, brushed his teeth, and got him dressed.

He had two suitcases: one for his clothes and one for his movies, magazines, and toys—packed mostly to comfort his mom and dad rather than himself. He hugged his brothers. They traded their secret handshake, and Jake offered a volley of hand-blown kisses in signature departure. Finally, he kissed his little sister Hope wetly on top of the head and gave her a slightly choking hug.

I was taken aback to see Hope cry that morning. I guess I never realized that her feelings for Jake went very much beyond frustration and fear. She was only three at the time, and since her adoption into our family she had never really seen the happy, animated, sparkling Jake the rest of us knew. But now there was an evident bond between them that I hadn't noticed before. There were many strong bonds on display that morning.

Kim chose to make the five-hour drive to The Potomac Center with her best friend, Kelly, while I stayed home with the other kids. As a mother, she needed to see where her son was going and meet the people who would be caring for him. Kim had been the one to take the reins and get Jake enrolled at the Center against all odds. She has always been Jake's greatest advocate, ensuring at each step along the way that his care has been all it could be. Her motherly love and devotion to this difficult child has been the closest thing to Christ-likeness that I have ever experienced in human form. She has been relentless in her commitment, dedication, and care for seventeen years.

I think it to be more providential than ironic that Kim's driving partner that day had also been instrumental in Jake's adoption. When Jake was a healthy but premature newborn in the NICU, Kelly was the first to encourage us to adopt him. She took the initiative to research the process and put us in touch with an adoption lawyer. She even became Jake's foster mom while we finalized the home-study portion of the adoption process. It's because of Kelly that we came to love the little red-haired boy who would change our lives for eternity. In my absence, I could think of no better person to make this difficult trip with my wife and son.

I buckled Jake into the truck, kissed him on the lips, and made him look me in the eyes. "I love you son. I love you more than you will ever know this side of heaven. Do you know that I love you?" He gave two quick nods of his head in a forward jerking motion, his usual sign of agreement. I closed the door and watched the truck drive away.

And just like that, he was gone.

✻ ✻ ✻

For the longest time, it was almost like there had been a death in the family, except no one showed up with food or condolences. I have never felt loneliness like I felt that first week. While it is true that sometimes God surrounds us with friends and family in times of hurt to help heal our wounds, it seems like in the most painful times—when the wounds are the deepest—He removes everyone else, so that He is all we have left to cling to.

I told a friend it was like Kim and I had just completed a marathon together, but when we crossed the finish line no one was there to cheer. Then we realized the race had been over for quite some time. All the lights were off and the crowds had gone home. There was no applause or celebration, just exhaustion, weariness, and fatigue. We embraced each other at the finish line knowing we had lost, but still grasping for some comfort in the fact that, at the very least, we had finished the race.

I really don't know where to go from here. Perhaps I'll get a hobby, go fishing, make some new friends and do whatever good friends do. Maybe I'll spend some quality time with my other three children, who have been so patient and generous with their dad's focus on Jake through the years. Better yet, I think I'll ask my wife out on a date, begin courting her again, and pick up where we left off—somewhere in the past, when all our hopes and dreams were fresh and new.

I knew that, whatever I was going to do, it would be very different than what I had done for the past seventeen years. Caring for Jake had formed my purpose and shaped my character for most of my adult life. This wasn't going to be easy.

❊ ❊ ❊

It's been a little over a year now since Jake left, and we have seen many simple yet profound reflections of God's grace as we settle into our son's absence. To lay in bed on a Saturday morning, to sit on the porch swing with my wife, to go fishing with my other sons, have a tea party with my daughter, or go out to a restaurant with the entire family—these used to be rare jewels of exceptional blessing. Now they are strangely normal. I can see how the average family could very easily take these moments for granted. I hope we never do.

We took a vacation this year and did things as a family that we have never done before. For three adventurous weeks we lived life daringly, almost recklessly, camping in a tent all up and down the East Coast. We drove nearly 4,000 miles, traveling back roads, hiking difficult trails, and learning deep things about each other. It was a glorious, magnificent time that provided grace and healing to our family as a whole.

For Jake, things have been even better. The Potomac Center has been a wonderful place of nurture for our son, providing him with the care we had always wanted to give, but could not seem to provide. To our joy and amazement, Jake has thrived in this environment. He has become toilet trained for the first time in his life and now sleeps through the night, something that rarely happened when he was home. He interacts well with the staff and other residents. He even dresses himself and takes showers. The specialized, structured routine the Center is able to provide has allowed Jake to develop skills we would have never thought possible.

More importantly, Jake is at peace. His personality seems to have returned and he is happy. For the first time in a long time, our son is happy.

Still, the sweet blessings of peace, tranquility, and answered prayer that have come to Jake and to us have a bitter side, too. Our family is incomplete. A son is missing. There is an empty chair at the dinner table every evening. His bedroom is vacant, the house is very quiet, and our lives have been changed dramatically.

Perhaps change is what grace is all about. We have entered a new season of life since Jake left, and this evening, through the open window of my study, I can hear the stream outside flowing hard against its banks, draining the surrounding hillsides saturated by the violence of yesterday's storm. But the rain has subsided and the sky is clearing tonight. The woods are alive with the sounds of late spring and there is a certain hope in the fragrance of the air. The promises of God's grace stand solidly before me as the assurance of His faithfulness rises with comfort behind me, fleshed out in the difficult life-lessons of my broken, disabled son. Only now do I understand that I have been the student and Jake has been the teacher.

Jake has taught me much about strength by displaying my utmost weaknesses. I have learned greatness by recognizing smallness, and learned victory by experiencing defeat. The painful death of personal pride has, perhaps, given birth to a simple humility. My own disabilities have been revealed through Jake's amazing life, and I have been shown that from *disability* God can create *depend-ability*, the strength that comes from admitting my own weakness and depending on Him who has all power.

All of these lessons have been studied in the shadow of the cross—the greatest display of victory over disability and weakness the universe has ever beheld.

But perhaps the sweetest discovery of all was learning more and more about the character of my heavenly Father through the struggles of my disabled son. It is one thing to read about His faithfulness, to talk about His mercy, and to write about His grace. But to experience these things face to face requires a heavenly vision that can only be obtained by walking through the suffering of His providence and coming to the realization that the darkness I have experienced is actually the shadowing shelter of my ever-present Father.

It is in this shadow that I have wrestled with an angel until the breaking of today. And even though I now feel beaten and broken from battle, the limp that carries me away from this sacred place forever reminds me that I have been touched by the hand of the Almighty. And by grace, I have prevailed.

Reclaiming Adoption
Missional Living Through the Rediscovery of Abba Father

Dan Cruver, Editor
John Piper, Scotty Smith
Richard D. Phillips, Jason Kovacs

"There is no greater need in our day than theological clarity. Dan has brought us near to God's heart. As you read this book, you will sense the need to embrace your own acceptance as God's adopted child."
–Darrin Patrick, Pastor and author

"I can't recall ever hearing about, much less reading, a book like this before. Simply put, this remarkable volume fills a much-needed gap in our understanding of what the Bible says both about God's adoption of us and our adoption of others. I highly recommend it."
Sam Storms, *Author of* The Singing God: Discover the Joy of Being Enjoyed by God

"The authors writing here are some of the most fearless thinkers and activists in the Christian orphan care movement. Read. Be empowered. And then join Jesus for the orphans of the world."
Russell D. Moore, *Pastor and author of* Adopted for Life

"With spiritual insight and effective teaching, *Reclaiming Adoption* will help believers better understand our place with Christ and work in His kingdom."
Ed Stetzer, *President, LifeWay Research*

"Something like...a revival, is happening right now in evangelical theology....it may have the momentum to reinvigorate evangelical systematic theology....The most promising sign I've seen so far is the new book *Reclaiming Adoption*.
Fred Sanders, Ph.D., Biola University

Intentional Parenting
Family Discipleship by Design

by Tad Thompson

The Big Picture and a Simple Plan — That's What You Need to Do Family Discipleship Well

This book will allow you to take all the sermons, teachings, and exhortations you have received on the topic of family discipleship, make sense of it, and put it to use.

"As parents, we know God has given us the responsibility to train our children in his ways. But many parents don't know where or how to start. Tad has done us all a favor by identifying seven key categories of biblical teaching we can utilize in teaching our children godly truth and principles. This easy-to-follow plan will help any parent put the truth of God's Word into their children's hearts."

Kevin Ezell, President, North American Mission Board, Southern Baptist Convention; father of six

"Here is a practical page-turner that encourages fathers to engage the hearts of their families with truth and grace. In an age when truth is either ignored or despised, it is refreshing to see a book written for ordinary fathers who want their families to be sanctified by the truth. Thompson writes with a grace which reminds us that parenting flows from the sweet mercies of Christ.."

Joel Beeke, President, Puritan Reformed Theological Seminary

"Need an introductory text to the topic of discipling children? Here is a clear, simple book on family discipleship, centered on the gospel rather than human successes or external behaviors."

James M. Hamilton, Associate Professor of Biblical Theology, The Southern Baptist Theological Seminary

The Organized Heart
A Woman's Guide to Conquering Chaos

by Staci Eastin

Disorganized?
You dont need more rules, the
latest technique, or a new gadget.

This book will show you a different,
better way. A way grounded in the
grace of God.

"Staci Eastin packs a gracious punch, full of insights about our disorganized hearts and lives, immediately followed by the balm of gospel-shaped hopes. This book is ideal for accountability partners and small groups."

    Carolyn McCulley, blogger, filmmaker, author of Radical Womanhood *and* Did I Kiss Marriage Goodbye?

"Unless we understand the spiritual dimension of productivity, our techniques will ultimately backfire. Find that dimension here. Encouraging and uplifting rather than guilt-driven, this book can help women who want to be more organized but know that adding a new method is not enough."

    Matt Perman, Director of Strategy at Desiring God, blogger, author of the forthcoming book, What's Best Next: How the Gospel Transforms the Way You Get Things Done

"Organizing a home can be an insurmountable challenge for a woman. The Organized Heart makes a unique connection between idols of the heart and the ability to run a well-managed home. This is not a how-to. Eastin looks at sin as the root problem of disorganization. She offers a fresh new approach and one I recommend, especially to those of us who have tried all the other self-help models and failed."

    Aileen Challies, Mom of three, and wife of blogger, author, and pastor Tim Challies

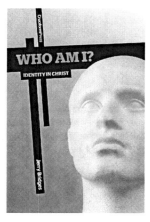

Who Am I?
Identity in Christ

by Jerry Bridges

Jerry Bridges unpacks Scripture to give the Christian eight clear, simple, interlocking answers to one of the most essential questions of life.

"Jerry Bridges' gift for simple but deep spiritual communication is fully displayed in this warm-hearted, biblical spelling out of the Christian's true identity in Christ."

> **J. I. Packer, *Theological Editor*, ESV Study Bible; *author*, Knowing God, A Quest for Godliness, Concise Theology**

"I know of no one better prepared than Jerry Bridges to write *Who Am I?* He is a man who knows who he is in Christ and he helps us to see succinctly and clearly who we are to be. Thank you for another gift to the Church of your wisdom and insight in this book."

> **R.C. Sproul, *founder, chairman, president, Ligonier Ministries; executive editor*, Tabletalk *magazine; general editor*, The Reformation Study Bible**

"*Who Am I?* answers one of the most pressing questions of our time in clear gospel categories straight from the Bible. This little book is a great resource to ground new believers and remind all of us of what God has made us through faith in Jesus. Thank the Lord for Jerry Bridges, who continues to provide the warm, clear, and biblically balanced teaching that has made him so beloved to this generation of Christians."

> **Richard D. Phillips, *Senior Minister, Second Presbyterian Church, Greenville, SC***

Grieving, Hope and Solace
When a Loved One Dies in Christ

by Albert N. Martin

**There is comfort for the grief.
There are answers to the questions.
The Bible does offer hope, solace,
healing, and confidence.**

**Pastor Albert Martin has been
there.**

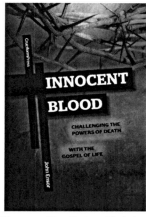

Innocent Blood
Challenging the Powers of Death with the Gospel of Life

by John Ensor

The shedding of innocent blood, primarily through abortion, has marked an entire generation.

Yet God's command to defend the innocent is unchanged.

We can obey that call.

"*Innocent Blood* brings Christians face to face with the horror of abortion and our responsibility to intervene. Better yet, by showing how our activism is to be motivated and fueled by the gospel, Ensor challenges us to devote our lives to magnifying Jesus Christ through seeking justice for the unborn."

> **Trevin Wax, author of Counterfeit Gospels and Holy Subversion, editor at LifeWay Christian Resources**

"*Innocent Blood* is a powerful indictment...The author presents many biblical passages that should constrain our consciences and our actions. There are areas of theology about which sincere Christians can disagree, but this is not one of them. The Scriptures are as clear as they can be that God's people have the responsibility to stop the shedding of innocent blood."

> **John Frame, Reformed Theological Seminary**

"Stellar! John Ensor provides a bridge between the defense of innocent human life and the proclamation of the gospel. His concisely worded thesis is theologically grounded, philosophically sound, and gives us the tools to engage the culture on the burning moral question of our day. I wholeheartedly recommend this book!"

> **Scott Klusendorf, speaker and author of The Case for Life: Equipping Christians to Engage the Culture**

Friends and Lovers
Cultivating Companionship and
Intimacy in Marriage

by Joel R. Beeke

Marriage is for God's glory and our good.

The secret?

Intimate Christian companionship.

"A book about love, marriage, and sex from Joel Beeke that is surprisingly candid yet without a trace of smuttiness. Fresh and refreshingly straightforward, this is the best book of its kind."

Derek W H Thomas, Visiting Professor, Reformed Theo. Sem.

"Marriage is hard work. And wonderful. And sometimes, it's both at the same time. *Friends and Lovers* is like a personal mentoring session on marriage with a man whose heart is devoted to seeing Christ honored in how we love each other as husbands and wives. It's full of practical wisdom and grace. A delight."

Bob Lepine, Co-Host, FamilyLife Today

"By laying the theological, emotional, social, and spiritual foundations of marriage before heading to the bedroom, Joel Beeke provides a healthy corrective to the excessive and obsessive sex-focus of our generation and even of some pastors. But, thankfully, he also goes on to provide wise, practical, down-to-earth direction for couples wanting to discover or recover physical intimacy that will both satisfy themselves and honor God."

Dr. David Murray, Professor, Puritan Reformed Theo. Sem.

"There is no better book than this to renew the affection of happy marriage."

Geoffrey Thomas, Pastor, Alfred Place Baptist Church, Wales

Getting Back in the Race
The Cure for Backsliding

by Joel R. Beeke

Backsliding is the worst thing that can happen to anyone claiming faith in Jesus.

Find out why. Learn the diagnosis. Experience the cure.

"This book is a masterpiece, and I do not say that lightly."
– *Martin Holdt, Reformation Africa South*

"An honest and sometimes chilling exposition of the seriousness of backsliding; at the same time, it unfailingly breathes the air of grace and hope. Timely and judicious."
> *Derek W. H. Thomas, First Presbyterian Church, Columbia, SC; Editorial Director, Alliance of Confessing Evangelicals*

"Too many modern Christians are opting for shrimpishly small degrees of grace. Indwelling sin drags the careless believer down into guilty backsliding. This book is a prescription for the believer who feels his guilt."
> *Maurice Roberts, Greyfriars Congregation, Inverness, Scotland; former editor,* Banner of Truth *magazine*

"This is a book for all Christians, certainly not only for those who are in the sad state of backsliding. Prevention is always better than cure."
> *Reverend Ian Hamilton, Cambridge Presbyterian Church, UK*

"Any of us may drop out of the race; Joel Beeke will help us prevent that happening by showing why it does happen and how it can be overcome. May this book help us to stay the course all the way to the finishing line!"
> *Iain D. Campbell, Minister; 2012 Moderator, Free Church of Scotland General Assembly*

"But God..."
The Two Words at the Heart of the Gospel

by Casey Lute

Just two words.
Understand their use in Scripture,
and you will never be the same.

"Rock-solid theology packaged in an engaging and accessible form."
– Louis Tullo, Sight Regained blog

"Keying off of nine occurrences of "But God" in the English Bible, Casey Lute ably opens up Scripture in a manner that is instructive, edifying, encouraging, and convicting. This little book would be useful in family or personal reading, or as a gift to a friend. You will enjoy Casey's style, you will have a fresh view of some critical Scripture, and your appreciation for God's mighty grace will be deepened."
Dan Phillips, Pyromaniacs blog, author of The World-Tilting Gospel

"A refreshingly concise, yet comprehensive biblical theology of grace that left this reader more in awe of the grace of God."
Aaron Armstrong, BloggingTheologically. com

"Casey Lute reminds us that nothing is impossible with God, that we must always reckon with God, and that God brings life out of death and joy out of sorrow."
Thomas R. Schreiner, Professor of New Testament Interpretation, The Southern Baptist Theological Seminary

"A mini-theology that will speak to the needs of every reader of this small but powerful book. Read it yourself and you will be blessed. Give it to a friend and you will be a blessing."
William Varner, Prof. of Biblical Studies, The Master's College

Lightning Source UK Ltd.
Milton Keynes UK
UKOW032046140313

207659UK00001B/5/P